Alone in the Dark

MY BATTLE WITH DEPRESSION

LATOYA NICOLE

ALONE IN THE DARK: MY BATTLE WITH DEPRESSION

ISBN PRINT:979-8-9857914-0-2

Editing Services by Adrienne Michelle Horn of I A.M. Editing, Ink

Photography by Eric Singleton

Graphic Design by freelancerguru222@gmail.com

www.latoyanicoleinc.com

Contents

Dedication

Cayla, I dedicate this book to you because before you knew what you were saying, messages were coming through you, encouraging me to write. You were a little girl saying almost every day, "Mommy, write a book." You were too young to know that it was my desire or how much I loved writing, nor did you know I did not believe I would succeed. But your constant reminders and the seeds you sowed landed on fertile soil, producing a bountiful harvest.

Preface

Depression is no joke, and it almost took me out before I realized what it was. An unknown enemy is far worse than one you can pinpoint. If I know what I am up against, I can combat it, but unfamiliar territory of this magnitude can leave you near death, crawling your way out.

This enemy will leave you wandering, starving, and desperate if you allow it to sink its grip too intensely. I hate it! What depression does to people, I hate it! It trapped me, unable to vocalize the pain without others saying crazy shit to me, and I hate that growing up in a black household meant that "ain't nothing wrong with you, what you got to be depressed about."

It sucks to feel all alone and misunderstood. You know something is off, but you can put your finger on it. It was hard reliving these experiences as I wrote. To go back to those times after I had cried them all out was not fun, but it had to be done. I needed to share my experience to bring awareness about how this aliment sneaks in and robs us.

I hear talk of proclivities all the time but hardly hear about depression. Our community is okay with saying, "That boy drinks just like his daddy," and not acknowledging he is battling depression like him. Being like our parents in these ways is not a flex, and we need to stop. People self-medicate for a reason; let's understand why and get them help before it is too late.

I am not a therapist. I am here to tell my story. Hopefully, the words you find here will lead you to the help you need. We are not being silent about this anymore. We learn the predispositions are the generational curses and that those codes unlock when lack of knowledge and circumstances marry to open them.

Fleeing Darkness

It is a fact that suicide has increased among black youth over the past 20 years. Sadly, black people are less likely to pursue treatment. It is too late when most realize they are experiencing depression. Black households do not acknowledge depression; it is called everything, making it hard to treat. This ignorance leaves many in the dark concerning their mental health. They do not know what to do or where to turn because seeking professional help labels them "crazy."

Have you ever heard the statement, what happens in this house stays in this house? Did you know that expressing how you feel is a sign of disrespect in some households? Have you ever tried taking your life and found yourself belittled for doing so? If so, your journey through this book will show you how damaging those things can be to a person's core.

I, too, have been there, and it was difficult to face each day. It seemed like every attempt to take my life failed. I seemed to have been the problem, and I tried to eliminate it. I grew frustrated because I would not die. Depression had become a part of me; I did not know myself beyond it. The thought of not having those bouts to look forward to was scary at one point. If you have experienced trauma, I encourage you to seek professional help. This does not mean you are crazy or weak. It means that you are strong enough to rewrite your story.

In this book, you will learn how sadness develops into depression when left untreated. When a person is sad, depending on how they respond can unlock depression's door. Those are the generational traumas that pass down in the womb from parent to child. As you read, you will learn of different holistic modalities that can help process emotions and heal core fractures. NO longer do you have to battle depression. Liberation awaits!

I battled depression for decades. One disappointing event after another, I spiraled out of control. I was locking myself in my room, bathing in tears. Like a turtle putting its head back in its shell, I hid from my pain and what caused it. My defense mechanism was to appear mean and aloof while I was so fragile that a single pluck would break me. I became the person collecting scars like they were a treasure. I did not know what to do with them but hide and throw myself pity parties every day. Yes, the way I felt was valid, but it served no purpose staying at the party for as long as I did. Isolating became my way of hiding from those who caused the pain until I was ready to present myself to the world again. I was so engulfed in this mechanism that it became a trap. A trap that grew harder and harder to break free from. It seemed like I dug myself a bottomless pit that I was now struggling to escape from.

As a Certified Belief Therapist and Life Coach, I help others peel back layers within my scope. My business successfully assists people in organizing in several ways, including emotionally. The same strategy I used today was the one that helped me. It is an honor to pay it forward by using my voice to share my life experiences in hopes it helps the next woman, man, or child out of their pits. Learn from my mistakes and refuse to hide; face yourself sooner than later.

I get it! Taking the cap off can be scary because there is no going back once it is off. Please do not put it off any longer. You have a purpose, and you have people to save that will be in the same place you are now. They will need you; they will need you free. No one wants a party guest at their lowest; they need your strength to help them to safety. Do you have children? How would you feel seeing them repeat the same cycles as you are? You want more for them, right? Well, decide now to heal.

As you adventure into the highs and lows through this book, reflect after each section and unpack. Decide to write a new story. Your wounds can help you grow if you see them that way. During the most depressive times in my life, I battled negative thought patterns, attempted to hide from the pain, and dwelled on what I could have done differently. I never felt so alone as I did then. Thinking I was the reason those around me were not happy made me want to give up on this thing called life. I do not want this to be you. I do not want you to feel defeated and want to give up on the purpose you entered this realm to fulfill. The constant mental torture I faced transformed me into an angry person; I exploded at whoever came my way for any little thing. This painted me negatively, and I grew up with a family that only expected me to have a horrible attitude. They can not receive where I am now in life because that is how they saw me and convinced others to see me. Knowing this only deepened the sadness I felt. Healing will not be overnight. Take this thing one day at a time; what I can say is that on the other side is the abundance of peace awaiting you, and I want nothing more than to see you dwell there.

So, are you ready? Are you prepared to go deeper? Are you ready to look at the examples enclosed and complete the prompts to unpack emotionally? Are you prepared to give voice to what is going on and heal? Are you ready to pray specific prayers and not those avoiding the issue? Are you ready for answers by way of action steps you can take? If so, keep reading; you are no longer Alone in the Dark.

CHAPTER 1

Undetected

I was nineteen years old and pregnant with my daughter when a medical professional prescribed me anti-depressants.

I recall seeing a school counselor in elementary, but I shut down on her after insinuating that I was the problem. The lady did not know what was going on at home, and she did not even care enough to ask. I felt what I said wouldn't matter at that point; she would dismiss me because the grown-up already thought I needed fixing. Back then, a child had no say, and whatever an adult said went. This ignorance continues today and results in more children wanting to shoot than talk.

There are adults by the droves toting around wounded children. Biologically, they are adults, but emotionally, they are seven years old. They are afraid to give voice to the pain because they feel it would disrespect those who sacrificed for them to be here or shed light on the source of the pain.

Some get help; most do not. In seeking help, there is an admission that something is wrong or that someone you are loyal to has wronged you. In my coaching business, I encounter adults who do not know how to use their voice, and the root cause is how they were told to "shut up" whenever they were trying to explain that pain. The classic "I am your mother; you will not speak to me in that way" is one of the many ways they silence children while trying to voice their pain.

Depression is not something spoken about in most black households. The signs and symptoms are clear, but we usually pass them off as laziness, a nasty attitude, or not amounting to anything. Thought labels like these only sink the person further into depression, primarily when these thoughts become words spoken during an already low point.

I pretended for a long time until I could no longer hold up the facade. I wore how I felt on my sleeve. When I was sad, everyone knew. Even with a smile here and there or uncontrollable laughter when someone told a joke, I still wanted to cry. I was depressed most of the time; I had hit rock bottom in my feelings, and life didn't seem worth living.

One of my classmates thought it was a great idea to tell everyone I took a remote across the face. The moment I stepped foot on campus, she approached me, asking if someone had hit me with the remote control. I was in disbelief that she knew that, but after learning, my brother told her it didn't surprise me. I never understood my classmates or my teachers. They thought it was funny; they never noticed the times I wore long sleeves in the summer or how withdrawn I got from time to time. I bounced from one end of the spectrum to the other; it was a rollercoaster of emotions.

As I watched and observed, I noticed a trend of depression within my family. They just called it something else. Had it not been for my routine checkups during pregnancy, I am unsure how long it would have taken me to figure out what was going on. My doctors prescribed me Lexapro, but I did not understand how a pill would help with emotional pain. Later in the book, you will read how I self-medicated to numb my feelings. I knew this pill would not help. There was something deeper going on, and a pill was not the answer.

We naturally release feel-good hormones, so if the medication contained synthetic dopamine, what could the synthetic chemical possibly be doing to our bodies? I learned so much over time about genetic structure; I use holistic methods to heal now as much as possible, not focusing on the chemical aspect alone. Our creator gave us everything we need to heal, prolonging life.

We can break generational cycles by simply educating ourselves further than what we learned in school. The depression symptoms I was experiencing went undetected for a decade. There was no help beyond the little offered by the pills, so eventually, I stopped taking them. I don't recall the doctor ever saying to talk to a mental health professional; the drugs did not change how I felt enough to justify taking them. If I had to take a medication every time I was sad, wouldn't that only create another addiction? I needed help, not an obsession.

Another decade passed before I saw a therapist, which was the best decision I made. Therapy helped me to understand the power I had. She was not an average therapist; she shot straight, making me snap out of my stupor. I could change by changing the way I saw the circumstances. I had the power to loosen my grip on the pain; it was almost as if holding on was some sort of badge of honor. I stopped beating myself up whenever I reached a low point. I could forgive and release people who were not adequately caring for me because no one did so for them.

Around the same time every year, I would sink into a worse state of sadness; every year, it was worse. I recall doing my cousin's hair at my apartment when I said those words, "I think I am depressed." I had not acknowledged that to anyone before that conversation. There was some relief in saying it aloud; however, recognizing it did nothing to spark the need to seek help.

I did not want to feel like that, nor did I want to replay every failure once more, possibly facing the loss again. I wanted to live out the things I dreamt about when I wasn't in this state. Each time I attempted anything new, it blew up in my face. I tried working with people, and of course, those projects did not last. Secretly, I began resenting women because they were the ones who hurt me as a child. The moment they presented themselves in my life, I watched and waited for them to show their true colors or display traits like my abusers, waiting for them to hurt me, waiting for me to cower and take cover.

In 2016, a flood swept through Baton Rouge, LA, claiming lives, property, and sanity for some. When the water rushed in, my daughter and I were in the house. Completely frozen in shock at what was happening, we almost did not make it out in time. I had just purchased the home one year earlier, so what was happening was too much, and I did not prepare. I was a single mother raising a child unknowledgeable about a lot. A relative was living with me during the time it flooded. They were not present when it happened, and I did not have time to think about saving a house filled with belongings. As a result, all of their things got destroyed, and somehow that was my fault. My daughter and I did what we could and got out of there; thankfully, we got out just in time because the water could have trapped us had we stayed any longer.

At the beginning of this catastrophic event, I felt fine, but it took a turn for the worse. My daughter was stressed, so I saw her behave in a way I never had before. I was worried, bouncing from place to place with constant thoughts of how I would recover. There was no time to rest. I know people say to take it one day at a time, but that was difficult for someone who overthought everything.

Being consumed with tomorrow was something I could not do away with after losing everything I worked so hard to get. People said some of the most insensitive things to me during that time. 'Be grateful' was one I grew tired of hearing the most because it did not change the loss I faced or lessen my burdens. Somehow, stating how you feel equates to complaining, and because of ignorance, people are put off and refuse to express what is bothering them or get the help they need. I was trying to be open about the feelings circling throughout my body, but the responses made me feel like my expressions meant I was not grateful to have lost everything except my life.

It was over a year later before I could accept my fate and move on concerning what took place. I enjoyed being alone in my space, so staying with other people took a toll on both my daughter and me. I was not happy with the treatment we received from some homeowners we encountered. The "I am doing you a favor mentality" and "since you are in my home, you will be at my disposal" mindset was enough for me. It reminded me too much of how people dismissed me when I had nothing to offer when I was younger. I was so tired, and I wanted to go to my house. We were not sleeping well, and besides that, family members were doing their best to bring me down further. I noticed how I'd only heard from them when things were terrible in my life, but not to comfort me, only to make them worse.

During this time, I realized certain situations dredged memories I had buried. I allowed the pain associated with the memories to create emotional chaos, resulting in a disorderly life. Finally, I was ready to get some help. I started seeing a professional two times per month for months before getting on a monthly schedule. I couldn't have made a better decision. Everything was surfacing, and I knew I needed to get some help. I was drowning in pain night after night, and it was filling my lungs at a rapid rate.

I needed to stop holding on to the past because it only made matters worse. I could feel the pain up to my throat. The pressure was building up, so I made a sound as I broke into tears to release it. Sitting on my bedroom floor, I screamed. I did not want to have to deal with any of it anymore. I was not too fond of it, nor did I want to be in that situation anymore. All the disappointments felt like daggers in my flesh; there were too many to count. I was sure I'd bleed out and die if I tried pulling them out. Therapy helped me get to the source of the daggers, extricate them gently rather than an aggressive pull because I wanted the pain to stop, which was the healthiest method.

Journaling had been something I had done for a very long time. I did not feel entirely safe because my family would read my notes and use them against me. As a result, I grew scared to write freely and only did it here and there until I was on my own. That provided enough release to keep me alive, and it made a tremendous difference when coupled with therapy. I was happy that my therapist recommended journaling to her patients and more traditional practices. That assured me I would be okay; I had already taken a step on the right path.

Every session peeled back another layer until I could finally stop holding my breath and feel a sense of relief. There were times we talked, times she allowed me space to cry uncontrollably, and times we prayed. Dr.

Green saw so much in me. She was the first to tell me I would become an author, apart from my daughter. She was the only one who seemed to believe in me. Unaware that it was a desire, I received it gladly. She was unaware that I started working on a manuscript during that time or that her kind words had motivated me to continue. I knew that was my sign to keep going.

Being picky about who I allowed in such vulnerable spaces also helped immensely. Some friends did not have the wherewithal to help with the pain that ran as deep as mine. Church leaders are not medical professionals; hearing what you discussed in your private sessions in next Sunday's sermon proves that. Medication will not make the trauma go away. Hence, the best route is to get therapy and a life coach to unpack your baggage and make some progress in your life. We quickly run to avenues that keep us comfortable in our pit. Your friends will tell you, girl; it will be okay, you doing what you have to do. Your pastor will say weeping may endure for a night, but joy comes in the morning. I learned people needed practical applications, not cliches and fluff. Many are sick because they attempt to hope the trauma away rather than seek help. For a long time, that was my mindset, and from my pain and experiences, I have learned strategies to help others. I use methods that will free people for real in my coaching practice. Second, you need to be honest, open-minded, and accountable. Healing is not pretty, and it will reveal the underlying horror. Refusing to do the work or holding back will only limit you.

Seeds planted in the soil of my mind before I was even born affected me. So, because of predispositions, I saw arrests, drug addiction, promiscuity, drinking, and emotional, physical, mental, and spiritual abuse roam throughout the walls. The walls were not just in my home but every wall within a dwelling I was ever a part of. We are the temple, so even within the confines of my walls, I lived out the very things I saw and hated about my upbringing. As much as I tried to escape, I could not run from what was inside of me.

Journal Prompt

Have you been sad for long periods? Can you identify what the onset of
the sadness was?

_____

_____

_____

_____

_____

_____

_____

_____

_____

_____

_____

_____

_____

_____

_____

_____

_____

_____

_____

_____

_____

CHAPTER 2
If These Walls Could Talk

The walls hummed to release the secrets they knew. While we grew afraid and hid, they were ready to talk.

Oh boy, where do I begin? Sadness is in the walls; trauma flows as a tub left running, pain circulates like the blades on a fan. The walls have collected the secrets. Walls there watching, listening, and they have a story to tell. Would the walls reveal the reason heads hung low, why nothing seems to work out, or who speaks ill of you when you are not present?

If walls could talk, they would expose people who pretend to have it all together; meanwhile, they mistreat their children. Those "I have a good heart" people would not be in the limelight if the community knew their heart was not pure towards them, and all they do is show them a facade because they need to be validated. Stories of favoritism, better yet, how the males could do no wrong while the girl's experience devaluing. Would the walls reveal emotional incest? Moms save their sons from wives who supposedly do not treat them right, while their daughters try to escape from a narcissist but are told, "He is a good man."

The walls in my childhood home could say a lot. Before I was born, those walls burned to the ground, taking with them decades of secrets, but the second home carried just as much pain. Remembering my childhood, I was sad most of the time. I thought it was normal to feel that way. At some point, the sadness slowly morphed into anger, all-encompassing anger that burned hot for everything in sight. It helped me remain in a world where I felt hated, but I was mostly unhappy with that life. There was a sadness in my eyes; some noticed and questioned it, but I never revealed the truth. I was not ready to open up.

One Christmas, I had on a green silk robe while I played with my Barbie stuff. I loved dolls as a child; they were perfect for playing teacher and living out my imagination. I got so many things that Christmas and wanted to play with them all, but I was told it could not all stay in the house. I had to pick one thing and put the remaining toys in a brown paper bag in the laundry room.

Back then, the laundry room was outside. I complied and took my toys out. I can't recall if the trash pickup was the next day or two days later. Back then, inmates picked up trash while the civilian drove the truck. Unfortunately, when I went to exchange toys, my bag was gone. I looked everywhere but could not find it, and I was throwing a fit. We later discovered that they picked my gifts up with the trash; the garbage is usually in black trash bags, not brown ones. When my mom took the trash out, she grabbed everything. As I got older, playing this story over and over, I felt like it was intentional.

I spoke about that incident during a coaching session over a decade later. My coach had me complete an exercise where I would buy myself gifts, wrap them, and have dinner as an adult. During dinner, I would open my presents and keep them. This activity flooded so many memories and emotions, leaving me weeping and unable to catch my breath. I did not realize until that moment how I held on to that and how much it hurt. After that incident, I got no more toys to replace what she took from me, and no one seemed to care. As much as people try to pretend they are okay, nothing hurts more than what your family does to you.

The walls of the apartment where I lived for a short period would tell how many times my aunt's boyfriend called me out of my name in anger and how I would not amount to anything because of what I watched on T.V. I was only a teenager. Even then, I wanted more, and I thought that moving away to live with them was the way to go, but boy, was I wrong.

In Madison, TN, at fifteen, I had a brush with death. I knew something was going on with me, but I did not realize the severity of it until I passed out in the middle of a hallway, unable to move; I was in so much pain. The doctor told my aunt I would not have made it if she had brought me a moment later. After spending several days in the hospital with a tube down my nose, I assumed I would go home to peace and relaxation, but it was the total opposite. I got back to rage, broken glass, and harsh words, which made me feel like I was the one that did something wrong. For most of my life, I believed that I was everyone's problem.

While I was in the hospital, management put an eviction notice on the apartment door. After experiencing something so traumatizing, I opened the door only to be traumatized again. The walls in my childhood home would speak to how we had to get out of bed at all hours of the night because one dish was in the sink, so this event was taking me on an unwelcomed journey back into the past.

After listening to my aunt's boyfriend rage, he forced me to clean up the entire apartment despite my near-death experience just a few days prior. I cried and cleaned up the broken glass he had shattered while he was livid. The tears did not stop for hours. I hadn't lived there long enough to be the reason for an eviction. However, I was still getting blamed for the problems the adults created.

So, here we are again, depression banging at the door, demanding to come in. I let it in, and it stayed until they sent me back to Mississippi for writing sexually suggestive letters to a boy I liked. No one back home knew what the boyfriend had done to me. They wanted me gone anyway, so the letters were the excuse they needed.

Those letters got me called whore, hit in the nose with a telephone as I attempted to call the police on my uncle, and sent to live with my father's mother. I wasn't sexually active with the man, but the way I wrote would have suggested otherwise. Everything I read in the novels made available to me I wrote about.

My uncle was justified in what he did and said to me.

I wondered how he knew what had happened. My aunt called and reported it to everyone who would listen. The world had to know of my transgressions. I had to have a letter placed on my chest and brought before the family for a verbal stoning. I do not recall any of the other cousins or my brother receiving such harsh punishment. They abused me for behavior I learned from them. I grew up watching people in my household change partners regularly; man after man and woman after woman was okay, but God forbid Toya, like a boy, or do the things I saw them doing. The nerve of me, learning from the examples presented.

I was a profoundly hurt child unless I was doing what everyone wanted. There were no conversations about boys, none about sex; hell, I learned about my period from a book. Why was I expected to be and do so much when there was not an ounce of guidance? It was okay for the man to tell me I wasn't shit and blame me for the entire situation if I said anything in my defense. I never understood my family's dynamic with men. I grew a resentment for any man whose family displayed the same tendencies as mine. Yes, I dated them, but I resented them.

There are situations where the walls would tell stories about jobs I've held, ministries I have been a part of, and organizations I have played a role in. The paint has stories—some occupants of said dwellings are bound to secrecy. The secrets have stagnated them, and they have taken residency in the cesspool of depression. Carry it to your grave; exposure is not an option.

"What happens in this house, stays in this house" is where the cycle of being bound by secrets formed. We learned that our voice and how we felt did not matter. Secrets destroy people as time passes, and they sit there stewing. The holder wants to release it but is too afraid to expose "family" because that is not loyal and goes against their forceful indoctrination. I've lived this and witnessed it. Statements such as these serve only to manipulate and control. Why can't someone report that their uncle is molesting them? Oh, because that would disgrace the family, or Uncle has to work and take care of his family. But the moment Uncle impregnates the girl, they force her to go away, abort her baby, or let her mother raise the child as hers. Why do we protect the predators the way we do? Where was this dynamic passed down from? When will it stop? Black families try so hard to appear right, morally wrong.

Are we not seeing what this is doing to children? Do we not realize the pain this causes and how it sends people over the deep end? They dwell on the past because it haunts them. The pain is loud, and it overpowers any sound they wish to hear. Nothing drowns it out or reduces it, so it gradually takes over. The depression grips them. As much as they want to fight it off, it is robust. Every time something terrible happens, it comes to collect. Things can go right for eleven months strong, but in the twelfth month, there are tests, and depression sinks its claws into you and snatches you again. Those automatic responses send you back into a deadly pit. The pit grows more complicated with each bout and becomes harder to get out of. It puts you to the test, and you fail every time because you cannot leave this toxic relationship.

Here is the trap!

What do you do? Each time is worse than before. When will it be the moment you cannot overcome it and successfully die? How do you break through? Why does it keep happening?

It has become a pattern. A vicious cycle of bouts of depression that leaves us unable to function in our routine day-to-day tasks is daunting. It will not leave you alone to move on or recover; it has to visit as often as possible. Tests come to see if you are healing or not. Opening your door and letting depression in once more means you are not growing or healing. As a result, it comes in and takes up residency like a relative who won't leave and eats up all your food. You do only what you know to do, give up. You stop your routine, you withdraw, you avoid people, and you sleep in the pitch dark. Your showers are now just to mask the tears.

Journal Prompt

What symptoms are you currently experiencing as it relates to depression? What are you holding on to that is causing severe sadness?

_____

_____

_____

_____

_____

_____

_____

_____

_____

_____

_____

_____

_____

_____

_____

_____

_____

_____

_____

_____

_____

CHAPTER 3
The Isolated Trap

Isolation is a dark place; trauma loves this place. No good thing is birth from being alone with negative thoughts.

Many go to this place and never return. It graced me to not only have made it out during one of my most challenging times but to write these words to help others avoid 'The Isolated Trap.' Never did I imagine what a detriment this pattern would be. Whenever I faced emotional setbacks, I did not know what it was doing to me mentally, physically, or emotionally. The last time was the last. It had to end; I wanted to be holy (WHOLE) more than I wanted anything else. Yes, to be holy only meant to be whole. Many are fragmented, hiding behind what they do, confessing holiness because they obey the commandments (I say this loosely). Still, the brokenness seeps through their pores. They are unyielding and refuse to heal from the trauma they've experienced.

"Be ye holy, for I am holy."

There is nothing fragmented about Christ, as this is a higher level of consciousness. The Bible says the veil was rent when He gave up the ghost.

According to Strong's Concordance H3354, rent translates as schizo; this is the root word for a word we know today as schizophrenia. Schizophrenia, in the simple term, means mental fragmentation. At the tearing of the veil, we can break free of what mentally fragments us by crucifying it and rising to Christ's consciousness. Is it not amazing realizing that the Bible talks about mindset? If we stopped reading it as a literal book, many would know these things and crack the codes instead. Reading it from a literal stance is why many battle depression and other fragments in their mind. We have the power to save ourselves, beginning with changing our mindset.

As early as I can remember, isolation has been my response when emotionally or mentally challenged. Anything that reminds me of negative experiences triggered me to run and hide and not come out until it was over. This retreat was internal and physical. Being abused and regularly lied about made me feel like everyone's problem. I felt misunderstood and could not express my feelings without harsh treatment, which left me unable to articulate what I truly felt, so I hid and wrote.

They snatched my power. I had no voice. It became next to impossible when I attempted to articulate my thoughts because I suppressed my emotions regularly. The loneliest place I have ever been in was where I was unheard and alone in the dark. It carried over into my relationships as well. I shut down when I experienced similar feelings from those I was with—severely depressed, which continued eating into my mind. No one saw me or heard the sounds of my tears dropping into the puddle I was now drowning in. Isolation did not seem like it was a bad thing. It was the only way to avoid being seen.

I felt it was a win-win since I enjoyed being alone and writing. It would be years before I realized how detrimental it was to isolate. The more I did it, the worse it got. There were times as a child I would sit in the closet playing with my toys, imagining a life different from what I had. Other times, I would go into the bathroom to run the water to mask the sound of my tears. Each drop seemed so loud to me, hitting the floor, but I did not want anyone else to hear it. During these times, I shut down emotionally and became numb. The pain I felt was like surgery without anesthesia. Even in my silence, it was so loud. My heart screamed for help, but no one heard me.

We create patterns when we do the same thing repeatedly. Some are okay habits to have, while others are a detriment. I would consider isolation a detriment. It's dark, cold, lonely, and hard to break free from. It was the way I responded that almost cost me my life.

When I hear others talk about their past, and they say, "I just wanted to be by myself," it makes me pause because I know what that feels like. We detour, getting off the main road, avoiding whatever caused the pain. Never challenging the root cause means we will never get rid of it. It was a dark road with few signs, no signal on a G.P.S., and street lights were all blown out.

Being by yourself is an "isolated trap," and the deeper we go, the darker it becomes, and we cut more off from society. Because of the twist and turns, it is hard to find your way to get back on track. Sometimes the light will shine, which will temporarily lead you back, but too often, the road is dark and will cause stagnation. The teacher will remain quiet while you struggle through the testing phase. I mean, you've gone over the information so many times. How can you not select the correct answer? It becomes a pattern; the test will become harder and harder to get out. You will feel like a character in the 'Wrong Turn' without shelter or weapons. You lose reception, your signal becomes weak, and you roam blindly to regain service.

Here we are again. Still denying the trauma, still not healing, still opting to take the dark road. Drifting deeper into the sunken place, I was lost, unable to find my way back. No service and out of gas. I was terrified.

Emotionally malnourished. I sat panicking because it trapped me again. The light was dim. It seemed blocked by my thoughts. I was all over the place, experiencing a range of emotions I had not before. Disappointment weighed too much for me to carry. There was no way out. I failed the test too many times. I was used to escaping before it consumed me, which made me immune. I expected to escape the trap as I had so many times before. Playing with fire will burn you. It was easy to slip in and hard to get out, but not this time. I had to work much harder than I ever had before. This time I thought I would die. I thought I would never make it out. There is no abundance here, only struggles. I lacked support physically, mentally, emotionally, and spiritually. I had no food to consume to regain the energy I lost fighting. The voices would not stop, and the thoughts of suicide increased. I had to deal with it all at once. All the once hidden pain surfaced; I would either succumb to it or process it. The choice was mine. Would I deal with the low self-esteem, the rejection, the emotional disasters, the self-sabotage, the destructive behavior?

Would I face this, or would I die?

The enemy that was my mind sought to devour me, consume me whole. Things that were said to me, coupled with what I saw, plagued my subconscious over the years and affected what I believed. It turns out it was dysfunction and self-limiting beliefs. I had lived in this space all my life. I made every decision from this place; the stagnation was birthed because of my time there. My urge to give up developed there; it was all birthed in this space. There was no outside entity doing this; the monster with horns did not exist. There was only me, my mindset, and my unprocessed trauma. That was my enemy. I struggled to deal with and face this enemy, so I regularly found myself in this place. I let this enemy win, which only made my visits more regular, making them worse each time to escape. This time, I had to crawl my way out. I had to posture myself on my hands and knees, crawling, screaming, begging for help.

I self-medicated, partied, smoked, drank, and sexed my way into an even more bottomless and isolated pit. At a crossroads of dwelling on what happened and worrying about what my future held, I started having panic attacks. I did not know what that was at the time until much later.

Anxiety and depression?

Those were my constant companions.

Then there was a mass on my pituitary gland. I was told it was why I experienced pregnancy symptoms when I was not pregnant. I self-medicated every opportunity I got. Even when I wasn't physically hurting, I was looking for a pill to knock me out in hopes I would sleep the emotional pain away. Imagine waking up only to find that what I thought was a nightmare was my reality. I'd become so addicted to coping because I did not know it could heal. It was my understanding that healing was just for wounds you could see, not those that were inside of me. I did not realize the scars inside of me had associated symptoms. Depression wasn't like having flu-like symptoms; these symptoms are much more subtle and not as easy to see, which is why they go undetected.

Journal Prompt

Do you feel alone?
Do you have anyone to talk to?
Have you sought help?
How do you feel at this moment?

_____
_____
_____
_____
_____
_____
_____
_____
_____
_____
_____
_____
_____
_____
_____
_____

CHAPTER 4

Medicating My Pain

I drifted off to a land that was free of all the pain. It saddened me to come back.

Medication does not heal. It relieves the symptoms for a few minutes and may even put you to sleep, but at daybreak, the empty feeling is back.

Medication was all I knew. Not just pills, but alcohol, excessive partying, and sex. I felt good, if only for a moment, but as with all medication, there were side effects. The effects of coping ushered me further into a space I did not want to be. Is this what rock bottom looks like? I often asked. It was so bad that if I missed a party, I would go insane. I thought I was being young and having fun, enjoying life. As much as I loved being alone, I loved to party too and would be mad as hell if I missed a night. Half dressed, attracting brokenness, it deceived me into thinking I was happy. None of it was helping. It only eased the pain temporarily. Those I hung out with stopped telling me where they were going because my dancing was so sexually suggestive that it took attention away from them. I was crashing and burning, and all 'my friends' could think about was men giving them less attention than they were giving me.

Pill popping became my thing; I did what I had to do to fit in and escape. I can't imagine how many teenagers are depressed and have resorted to self-medicating. How many parents assume it is just a phase they go through, never seeking help? What is this phase stuff about? Why are they all destructive? Are there any healthy phases to experience? We normalize these patterns by calling it a thing people go through.

Anything I could get my hands on to knock me out, I took it. I wanted to sleep it all away. I did not want to feel it anymore. The pain medication got me so high that I went numb. I loved the feeling. It made me tired, but it intensified the high, mainly when I fought the urge to go to sleep. I did not think about anything except the numb tingling feeling as I floated away from my pain, if only for a moment.

When I was high, I did not care what I did or said to anyone, especially my family. In my mind, cursing them out was what they deserved, but it only made things worse. I have the type of family who holds everything against you, no matter how small or petty. All of your low moments are ammunition for them. Once I had favorable moments, like succeeding at something, they would remind me of my low moments to bring me back down to their level. I allowed them to do it until I had had enough and cut them off.

There was a time I drank so much that I blacked out. A few people had me in a chair when I came to, fanning me, asking if I was okay. I did not recall what happened between the last cherry bomb and me regaining consciousness in that chair surrounded by people begging me to snap out of it before they put me outside. My inability to recall what happened was frightening. I sat in my room for days after trying to remember my steps, but I got nothing.

A guy I was interested in at the time told me he overheard plans some others had made to rape me that night. Of course, I questioned if anything had happened, but he was unsure as he had left moments later. I was not sore or anything, so I assumed my friends finding me was my way of escape. He had always been a sweet guy; I was just too messed up to realize it. I heard him loud and clear, though, so I stopped drinking that heavily. He did not know how appreciative I was of him, although I pretended like I had it all together. In my experience, it always took drastic things happening for me to come to my senses. I'm glad I did so before things took a turn for the worse.

The state of my emotional well-being had a scent. Those I attracted and chose treated me like I was never good enough. Same script, distinct faces. I would be well in my thirties when I learned most of them were narcissists and what they'd done to me was abuse in another form. Abusive people attached to me like a magnet. It was not what I wanted, yet I kept choosing it. Of course, the behavior was not obvious, but once it became apparent, it took me too long to let go. As crazy as it sounds to some, those relationships helped me heal in areas as I could see myself. They continue to and can for you if you see them for what they are. My inner child wounds were deep, and my relationships revealed such.

Sex was an outlet for me and a way to connect. In relationships, I felt alone, but connecting on that level made me feel like everything would be okay. My partners spoke to me in ways I could not believe. Trust me, I talked back, but only when provoked. One guy, in particular, left me flabbergasted; I tried to open up to him about the pain I was in. He listened and comforted me, but he threw it all in my face when it was beneficial to him, claiming I needed help. Having my pain weaponized silenced me even more. I did not want to talk to anyone about my feelings for a while. Little did I know he had childhood traumas as well that he had not processed. He would get high all day and not care about himself or his children, proving that he was as deeply depressed as I was.

It was one wrong decision after another with men. The moment they found a crack to get in, they did; I gave them all of me. Each one took a piece of me until I had nothing left. I wanted to experience a love so severely I accepted anything. Oddly, I thought I would find something when I was not aware of what it was. No one told me I was beautiful growing up, so they had me there. It was yet another vicious cycle that I thought would bring me some type of hope.

I often say that coping is popular; healing is not. The way I medicated my pain was only a coping mechanism I witnessed as a child. The things we do are familiar to us. In yielding to what's expected, we unlock the predisposition, which is the beginning of generationally affecting the bloodline until someone stops it. What our parents failed to heal becomes our cross to bear. Who takes time to see themselves and heal? I talk about healing a lot now. My voice is the power I have to create change, so I use it. Many did not know my story. My classmates did not see a depressed wounded person; they just saw a regular girl doing crazy shit. My family did not see a broken, depressed person; they saw a girl with a careless attitude whose choices would be a stumbling block for her.

I was so tired of them saying this crap. My attitude hindered them because they could not control me once I turned it on. The guys I dated or just had sex with did not see the scars; maybe they didn't want to. They only saw a girl who allowed them to get off. I did not have an orgasm until I was in my thirties, so yes, only they got off. I was chasing a feeling I read about in Zane's books, but I never came remotely close until I was older. Fulfillment in that capacity may have helped to a degree. I may have experienced some benefits, considering orgasms have health benefits, but even in that regard, I was unlucky.

We have to slow down long enough to take a long hard look at ourselves and be willing to fix those parts that do not benefit us. When we stop worrying about how others feel and allow them to be uncomfortable as we heal, we can break free. You may lose some people along the way, and it hurts so bad when you do, but all that proves is that those attachments were not healthy in the first place if they loosen because you are healing. That only shows someone was benefiting from you being in the shape you were in.

You are worth the effort it takes to heal and restore what you have lost. Do you think your creator made you to suffer, be without, and not fulfill your mission? Absolutely not! I know it is cliché, but you have a purpose, so whatever you need to do to tap into it, do it. Please do not wait another day or for approval from people who do not know themselves; make a move for you.

I have a daughter, so I had to do differently because she watched just as I watched my mother. Children see us, how we respond, what we do, how we say one thing and do another. We are our children's first teachers, and they apply what they learn. I thought I hid from my daughter, but she was watching. As a baby, she knew when I was sad because she only offered me her nook during those times. When my daughter turned 15, I got a bird's eye view of exactly how much she saw of what I thought she did not see.

Journal Prompt

How are you improving your situation?

_____
_____
_____
_____
_____
_____
_____
_____
_____
_____
_____
_____
_____
_____
_____
_____
_____
_____
_____
_____

CHAPTER 5

History Repeated

How could I assume removing her from the environment would change anything when I did not alter the environment within?

2020 was the year I had so much success and a massive threat to my emotional well-being. I began dating again three years prior after being single for ten years. I stopped for ten years for so many reasons. I was tired of being hurt, and I was unclear about what I wanted. I thought it was the right thing to do, considering I came second to men growing up, and I assumed time would heal me. As they say, time heals all wounds. In my trauma, I responded by devoting myself to my child, which was the mistake that caused the breakdown in our relationship. I had no balance, and that cost me.

I noticed my daughter got more and more unorganized. I was receiving backlash because of her mistakes, and I had enough. At 13, I saw a gift in her. She loved the kitchen, and she loved to bake even more. Cayyy's Creations was born soon after. I watched my daughter build her home-based bakery better than most adults. But she wasn't an adult; she was a child who had hit a phase where she wanted to explore other options. She was a child that I was proud to call my own.

My daughter did not know how much she helped me by living her dream. However, she grew tired, and rather than saying so, it showed up in her quality of work, and the first way of escape she took it, even if it was to my detriment. She did not state she needed a break, although I asked repeatedly.

The problems never ceased! If it weren't family members saying I was stealing her money, they would accuse her of using cheap products. There was more negativity from them than there was encouragement. Her behavior was triggering me left and right. I tried to use techniques I learned in therapy to maintain the peace, but it felt like something was trying to come up, and I needed just to let it out. I wondered if it was another form of healing, so rather than try to find a balance, I yielded and allowed it to keep happening with no resolution. It was a ride I rode for nearly a year.

I was so stressed; every time I went on a date, the conversation would be about how things were going at home. It wasn't enjoyable. One night, in particular, I stayed out as late as I desired. I needed to let my hair down, but my child found it necessary to call everyone who would listen to tell them I was not home. It only grew worse from there.

A case was already being built against me so that everyone could confirm I was the devil my mother told them I was. She had an army with her, but I was up for the fight. I've stood alone all my life, so this was not new to me. I saw the awakening coming, so as much as it hurt, I did what I had to do. Every day, I felt like I was in a boxing ring, and my contender was a part of me that needed to come out of hiding.

I saw all the signs, so I immediately sought counseling for her. Initially, it was hard to find someone to see her based on the limited help from our health plan, but they assisted me until we found the service we were looking for. By the time the first session came around, my daughter had decided she was moving out. It would take moving mountains any other time to get her dad to help her, but when I was the common enemy, he was right there by her side. She left to stay with him, but a few days later ended up with one of her aunts in Mississippi.

I saw a therapist as well, and she directed me to do activities. I sent one to my daughter via email, but she never got it. She missed her counseling session because the same aunt who withheld the email told her it was unnecessary to talk to people about her business. It was okay to say things to them, but not a professional. It was okay for her to have them conclude I was a lousy parent and leave it at that, but not talk to a professional who would help her navigate her feelings and get to the source of them.

There I was, making efforts to get my daughter set up with the family counselor while my family blocked it. She refused to see or talk to anyone because of what she was told. My daughter was so fragmented; she would have listened to and believed anyone who had something negative to say about me. I did not know what to do anymore and her leaving my home for good seemed like it would be best. I could no longer take the stress of what was happening, and it was affecting my health.

When she was away, my aunt sent me messages telling me why everything was my fault. It was one of the most challenging times of my life; it felt like everyone was stoning me. If I were not mentally stronger, I would have had a complete breakdown. On one end, I chose a man over her, and on the other, I should have talked to her about me dating again. I thought this was why I closed myself off from people. People say the stupidest things at the worse times, especially church people. They make everything religious, and I was over it. From that point on, I chose to only communicate with my therapist about what was taking place in my life.

When I convinced her of the importance of seeking outside help to navigate what we are individually and collectively going through, I found that my aunt's words weighed more than mine; she completed a session but did not like the counselor and refused to log on to continue. I found another one she seemed to love.

The counselor wanted to speak with me after the session only to tell me I had made wrong decisions and needed to make some changes to rectify the situation. I am a counselor, but I do not counsel my child; however, I could see more going on within her than me living my life. That may have been hard for her, but that was not it. It behooved me that no one was trying to figure out the root of the matter. It appeared her inability to articulate her feelings resulted in me becoming the primary target, and everyone she spoke with soon followed suit.

I was also sixteen once, so I know that when a sixteen-year-old hits this phase, their mothers become an issue. Where was this ideology when I was sixteen? It was never my mother, just me and my poor attitude. Funny how things change.

I admitted a lot. I attempted to raise a child in my brokenness, and I shut my life down, making her think my desires did not matter and that my entire life revolved around her. Although I was an adult, emotionally, I was still seven years old because my little person broke around that age. Seven-year-old Toya had a baby and bonded with her. When little Toya started reconnecting with big Toya and healing, a lot changed in my life. I apologized for my decisions and explained that I was not the person I was before because I was healing. I did my best to get my point across, but none of it was enough. She was experiencing a state of depression and confusion that caused her to want to destroy me. Through it all, I had to keep in the forefront of my mind it was not personal.

We all respond in different ways when depression knocks at the door. She targeted me while I targeted myself. She and her friends talked about me, her dad, my family, and family members' spouses. Everyone believed the worse. One of my cousins, who never calls me, did so during this time, crying and begging me to let her move to New York with her so that she could be safe. I was in such a state of shock that I could hardly speak. If you can paint a picture of a monster, this is what my so-called family thought of me. The actual monsters are never called out, though.

What in the hell was she telling these people was all I could think?

These people were around us. They talked to her on the phone all the time. What about the business I built, for God's sake, but to tell them I was abusive was believable? I did not pawn her off on anyone. I did not leave my daughter to be raised by someone else like I was. Considering I had no role model or help, I put my best foot forward. They knew what they did to me, which is why they believed the lies. After seeing cycles repeat themselves for so many generations, what made me different?

I was no longer parenting from pain, letting her have her way because I did not want to lose my friend. I was her parent, so that equated to abuse. The way her friends spoke was appalling. They once broke bread at my table. My child talking trash about me to her friends was heart-breaking. Her dad was absent; he did what he wanted when he wanted, yet he had an opinion about how I lived my life, having taken care of our child alone for all these years. I could not celebrate my best-selling author status because I was nursing wounds resulting from the constant assaults on my character. They all formed a line to shoot their shot; it felt like they had been waiting for the moment to do so.

When people cannot bring you down any other way, they will go through your children. My daughters' spirit mirrored mine at her age, and the only thing anyone did to help her was to assassinate my character because destroying another person makes them feel better.

No one talked to her about closing her business, her grades falling, the weight she gained, how she always stayed in the dark, how she slept all day and would do nothing I asked, how she spoke rudely to me every chance she got, etc. I was the bad guy suddenly. Allow me to impart some knowledge if you are a parent reading this.

If you know someone who does not like you, keep your children away from them. It is not safe! The village is toxic and will attempt to destroy you because they are bitter and disappointed. Jealousy and envy will bring out the worse in people, so protect your mental and your children. Also, start healing. I talked to my daughter at every phase of my evolution, I made it a habit of chatting with her every day.

Maintain balance! I was single for ten years for the wrong reasons, and it accomplished nothing. I came out of hiding but was still falling for narcissistic men. Take yourself out, learn about who you are and what you like, try some self-discovery; uncover who you are at your core. You owe it to yourself!

Journal Prompt

What are you experiencing? Did you see it growing up?

_____

_____

_____

_____

_____

_____

_____

_____

_____

_____

_____

_____

_____

_____

_____

_____

_____

CHAPTER 6
Church Tales

I thought this was where I would receive salvation, but I learned I had to save myself.

Religion is NOT an escape! It is not what you do to avoid working on yourself; it is not a quick fix—learning scriptures and dancing and shouting are not equivalent to healing. For some, it has become a form of A.A. You have your services, repent, and come back for more week after week, putting forth no effort to change. Is there real change week after week, or do we become disciplined and only show up out of fear of going to "hell?"

I have only been a part of two ministries, and I will share my experiences with both of them equally. Every stop on the path I chose, I will honor it, but people must understand that they have to work out their soul's salvation. Save yourself!

How many have waited and died waiting because it never came?

Myles Munroe said it best. "Everything we need is already in us."

The day I heard him say that while studying his teachings on YouTube changed so much for me regarding my healing journey. I wanted to know more about what he said; it's already in me. So, if it is already in me, why do I search outside of myself for it? My wheels turned at the thought, and I wanted to know more. I studied more than ever, and the knowledge I gained in my studying caused me to break free even more.

Are you aware that people put themselves in a depressive state because they either miss church or cannot afford to pay tithes?

I used to get down about not having money to raise a child with only minimum wage and no outside help. I had no support, meaning no family, no EBT, and an inconsistent baby father. Years later, I realized what I was doing to myself, but I learned that not giving to God puts curses on us. Yes, paying others' bills and not my own would keep me from being condemned. However, if I did not pay my bills and came home to no lights, that felt more like a curse.

Being active in ministry while still battling depression was hard. My pastor released words to me often. At one point, I was receiving a message from him every Sunday or Tuesday for weeks. I was so focused on the battle that I did not fully embrace what was imparted.

When God spoke about me purchasing a home, that one penetrated because I was praying to move out of the apartment complex I had stayed in for years. I took home buyers classes, devised a plan, and saw it through. Looking back today, that was what I missed all the other times, doing the work! People need to know the truth; the word of knowledge tells you that your creator has your back now, so execute.. Don't wait on anyone to give you the go-ahead; that was your go-ahead. Had I embraced every personal message the way I did this one, I would not have grown depressed when things were not happening. I had not activated faith to do the work, so I missed out.

I began sinking deeper as I faced mistreatment that mimicked my upbringing. Questioning my roles, I struggled to maintain what I needed to prove my faithfulness. There was a strong feeling that it was not for me; I did not know what I wanted. I felt better about myself and my life when I was not participating. Still, I allowed others to talk me into being active, as it would sharpen "the call," or I would join social circles within the church because I wanted to belong.

Early on, at the hands of female congregation members, they reminded me of the women I left behind in Mississippi. When I joined Grace & Mercy, I was so hungry to change and be a better person. I did not realize I was people-pleasing when I offered my services to the church because I was not working to pay tithes; I organized the store for free. My being there upset other people who were already volunteering there, and that's when the drama started. Of course, I had not healed my traumas, so I spiraled and got away from them when the mistreatment started.

I joined because I thought it would put me in a better emotional space, but it did not. Other congregants said things to me, making me feel like I was the problem. Before moving to Louisiana, the pastor's wife told me I would bring curses on my daughter and myself because God would have no one leave a Spirit-filled ministry to go somewhere else.

Those that had gone before me misinformed me about church. I thought I would get help, but I felt the same about life. After opening up a little, it hurt me, and I slipped even further into the mindset that I could not trust women.

After spending 12 years in ministry, it was not until I stepped away to seek what was within, I overcame the low state I had been in for too long. The church did not teach me inner work. It taught me how to cope and seek answers outside of myself. Religion taught me how to give my way through, praise my way through, get involved with many activities, not realizing that is a trauma response. I learned how to dress it up and look more presentable while crumbling internally. I was dying a slow death.

People knew I was desperate, and they tried taking advantage of me at every turn. When I did not conform, I became enemy #1. Church taught me that even if you are not the problem, you are not a favorite either unless you grew up in the ministry or had money. A minister pointed her finger in my face and told me what I would do. After several warnings to get her hand out of my face, I walked away and told her where to get off, but when it got back to leadership, she spun the story so well I was "rebuked" and told to check my fruit. If sabotage had a face, it was hers. The entire time I worked with her, that was her goal.

There I was, not fully healed, all while experiencing emotional and mental abuse at church. That was a difficult position for me to be in. What I imagined church to be was nothing like I imagined. I did not grow up in the ministry, so I did not know how it worked. I learned the hard, uncomfortable way.

During another incident, they likened me to a demon because I had enough and stood up for what was right. I was beyond tired of narcissistic leadership. That wasn't the most challenging part, though; what made it so hard was that I was the only one speaking up, which killed my case. There I was, the least favorite with so much stacked against me while trying to speak out against people whose leadership was mentally catastrophic. How they oppressed people was no secret, especially if you were not their top pick. People knew and allowed it because of their position, what they did for the church, and money. I had neither, and I was tripping, thinking anything would change. They had been doing that for years; nothing I said would change anything at that point.

If you refuse to be controlled, you are the problem!

In one group, there was so much breakdown in communication that leaders were told my attitude was a mountain that God had to bring them over, as it says in the song "For Every Mountain." No one ever asked me for my side; I was just told to "shut up." It amazed me how people stood proudly in error.

Leadership distastefully handled the situation. I learned about entitlement during that season and how easily people will discard you if you are not part of their crowd. The entitled had so much power; it was over for you if they got to the pastor first. If you do not stroke egos, your place to the entitled is but a vapor. It is more mess at church than you know. It isn't until you realize that there are unhealed messy people there— emotionally confused people who wear titles that are then used to abuse people. All of that chaos stems from their unhealed wounds.

I cringe when I hear people say that the church is a hospital; I worked at a hospital; sick people are there, some get out, some die. Is anyone genuinely healed at a hospital? They may ease their symptoms a little, but there are side effects to that. To further drive my point home, the etymology of hospital means to entertain, and the etymology of church is a circus.

My coach always says words are spiritual containers, so if you confess that "you are the church," please stop it; it may be one reason there is so much internal chaos. Have you ever visited a circus? And to say the church is a hospital, understand the definition because that is precisely what it has become. All of us who took part in releasing those frequencies thank yourselves for the state of the church because we do things in ignorance. Refusing to study anything beyond a book with thousands of translations, how do we know what was initially said?

While active in ministry, I wanted to kill myself. The state of my mind was far worse. I am not encouraging you to leave your church; I am asking you to get additional help because the church is not a therapist and will not help those traumas you need to overcome. Being holy is about being devoid of mental fragmentations; how can this be possible for someone who has not processed the pain that led them down depression lane? It is not a dress code or an amount of money; it is removing the veil from your mind so that you can walk into higher consciousness.

Do not feel bad for doing what you have to do for yourself. Saying no when you cannot make an event is healthy. Suppose you do not conform to their ideologies that does not make you a bad person. It means you are awake; you choose to think for yourself, and you decide to activate that single eye Jesus spoke of in Matthew 6.

See, the translators did a great job hiding the truth from us and making us get on one accord with things that keep us mentally fragmented and battling psychosis, but if you study and crack the codes, you will awaken and see. Seek professional help; We cannot pray away everything. Alter call will not uproot twenty-nine years of trauma; please seek help so that you can truly break free.

Journal Prompt

Are you a religious person? How have your beliefs helped or hindered your progress?

_____

_____

_____

_____

_____

_____

_____

_____

_____

_____

_____

_____

_____

_____

_____

_____

_____

_____

CHAPTER 7
Breaking Free

The grip tightens because we choose to hold on to what we should let go of because it is familiar.

I encourage seeking professional help if you have thoughts about harming yourself or others. In addition to professional services, there are other ways I could recover from decades of self-sabotage. Disappointing experiences leave us extremely sad, and those feelings affect different areas of life. We can, however, heal it through acknowledging, accepting, and processing it. It will not feel good as you face those things that want to keep you bound and stuck in depressive cycles. However, it is worth it.

Withdrawing became a significant problem as it developed into something medical professionals label as depression. Not all cases of sadness mean someone is experiencing depression, considering that sadness is a normal reaction to unpleasant circumstances. Prolonged sadness can lead to depression, which has far-reaching effects on someone's life.

I pride myself on doing something positive to improve my situation when I feel sad, and in doing so, I have made my life so much better. I went from listening to sad music, which feeds the sadness, to meditating, going for walks, playing tennis, or listening to music that gets me dancing. Your response will make or break you.

Journaling is my go-to; it helps me express how I feel, determine why I think the way I do, and work on the root cause. Many factors in our lives cause grief – relationship issues, financial problems, and even parenting. Besides situations such as these, I had accumulated pain from my childhood, which was taking its toll. I had to stop denying it, understand its effect on me, and change it.

Healing began when I put forth the effort. I made investments and stopped being afraid to look at who was in the mirror. Facing LaToya meant taking accountability for all of my flaws, stinking thinking, and poor decisions. Finally, I put my well-being first. I was not suitable for anyone, if not for myself. How could I love anyone or know what that looked or felt like if I did not first love myself? I needed to look in the mirror every day and love who was looking back and be proud of her. The best thing I did for myself, and you can do for yourself, is to free yourself from the negative thoughts you agree with. That may not be your truth. Every terrible thing said about me I believed became an agreement, which governed my life. Being called dumb, a female dog, or being told that I would be nothing or that I would never change played on my mental. I internalized it; the seeds took root and produced things I did not want. There was a chant I learned as a child: "sticks and stones break bones, but words never hurt." That chant was the ultimate lie. Words do hurt, and they affect our lives for generations as we emulate that behavior and pass it on to our children; this will continue to be the case if we do not change the narrative. Words are weapons that cause further damage to the core fracture of individuals. Admitting the words hurt may jumpstart healing for some.

Say it out loud, "What you said hurt me."

You must acknowledge it. Trying to bypass this step will not get you far, as this is the beginning. Think about it this way. When you go to the doctor, the first thing they have you do is confess the problem. You tell them what is wrong and then make your way from there. Life is no different; take that first step towards a more whole you. So, get that journal and write how you feel. A voice recorder does the trick as well. Whatever you have to do, get it out of your system. Unexplained pains could result from holding on to hurt. Imagine your food not digesting. It will rot in your gut, creating various ailments. Unprocessed pain does the same. Take care of yourself.

Breaking free entails studying beyond what someone says. I learned to think independently, tap into my inner knowledge, and trust myself. Breaking free was severing ties to what kept me in the dark; it meant leaving people behind that were vested in my demise. I had to learn that love would not do what they had done to me, even when I did it to myself. I was not obligated to my family if they mistreated me and devalued me every chance they got. In my learning, I broke free. I broke free of religiosity that kept me asleep. It was in my breaking free that I awakened. Breaking free from the pit does not mean I will not experience sadness; it means that I can quickly find my center and move to the other side of my problems without falling into darkness.

The more self-aware I became, the more I realized my internal chatter was the root of the sadness I experienced. What I said to myself and my thoughts caused most of my suffering. Yes, things happened to me. Yes, I was a victim, but I did not have to maintain that mentality. I imprisoned myself, and while in prison, it was dark and lonely, which produced the depressive nature which gripped me like a straitjacket.

The holistic modalities I used to release the disappointments and find balance in my life have helped me stay free from the trap's grip that almost claimed my life several times. Life happens, but life does not depress me anymore. Meditation, journaling, sunbathing, and letting people go who feel that I am their problem are some things I did to get to this point. We have to be okay with switching up what does not serve us. Shake the fear and what you think others will say or think and focus on what you need to better yourself.

As I continued my journey, I realized maintaining a relationship with my family was not the best decision. Being on a track to maintaining my mental and emotional health, I did what was best for me. I ended all communication to detach and find peace. While my daughter and I are back on track, there are individual layers we continue to heal. We are open with one another and upfront about how we feel. In our parent-child relationship, we have established boundaries.

Our relationship lacked one thing before; we did not respect one another. She is no longer an emotional support system for me, and I no longer expect her to be my adult best friend. Healing is beautiful when embraced. I've never felt this great or had a positive outlook on life, and it gets better day by day. Do what you need to do for yourself unapologetically.

Journal Prompt

Are you ready to break free?
What does removing the chains look like for you?

_____

_____

_____

_____

_____

_____

_____

_____

_____

_____

_____

_____

_____

_____

_____

_____

_____

_____

_____

_____

Ways I Overcame Depression

I learned the difference between depression and a bout of sadness.

I traced the origin of the depression.

I took accountability for my role in my life experiences.

I sought professional help.

I stopped expecting more from others than I did for myself.

I released how I felt about things by journaling.

I started meditating daily for at least five minutes.

I discovered new passions.

I turned my attention to a solution rather than dwelling on the problem.

I intentionally cried as often as possible.

I reframed negative experiences.

I forgave myself and those who hurt me.

Affirmations

I Am not alone.

I Am healing.

I Am abundant: mentally, emotionally, physically, and emotionally.

I Am valuable.

I Am love.

I Am worthy.

I Am intelligent.

I Am evolving.

I Am confident.

I Am getting stronger daily.

I Am not afraid of protecting my peace.

I Am okay with detaching from what is not serving me.

I Am proud of myself

I Am unapologetic about the path I have chosen to self-discovery.

I Am ready for a new way of thinking.

I Am my biggest supporter.

I Am powerful.

I Am seeing my circumstances from a different perspective.

I Am living my life by design.

I Am my help.

I Am rewriting the narrative.

I Am healing my children's children.

I Am WHOLE.

Reflection

_____
_____
_____
_____
_____
_____
_____
_____
_____
_____
_____
_____
_____
_____
_____
_____
_____
_____
_____
_____

REFLECTION

REFLECTION

REFLECTION

_____
_____
_____
_____
_____
_____
_____
_____
_____
_____
_____
_____
_____
_____
_____
_____
_____
_____
_____
_____
_____
_____
_____
_____
_____
_____
_____
_____
_____
_____

Acknowledgments

I would like to acknowledge We Dare Squad for their role in my life and for assisting me in finding and being comfortable using my voice. Thank you for teaching, encouraging, inspiring, and motivating me. When I was afraid because of my strong country accent, you pushed me, setting me free. I would not be where I am without the help of each of you.

.

About the Author

LaToya Nicole, a multi-talented, Bestselling Author, is also a Certified: Therapon Belief Therapist, Life Coach, Journal Therapist, Mindfulness Coach, and Business Coach. LaToya is also a Professional Organizer and creator of S.O.L.O. Coaching & Consulting, L.L.C., in Baton Rouge, Louisiana.

Eight years of leadership in the medical industry as a Community Health Worker for United Healthcare's Specialty Health Care Needs population reaffirms LaToya's dedication as she assists members with the effective utilization of individualized care plans.

As the creator of S.O.L.O. Coaching & Consulting, LaToya curates plans that allow clients to enhance their lives in a meaningful and authentic way. Relentlessly intuitive, LaToya develops purpose-driven paths that are beneficial and practical.

Highly approachable, LaToya understands the importance of emotional intelligence and optimal mental health and provides impressive insight rooted in her education and success in overcoming life's challenges.

In her personal life, LaToya achieves the balance of good mental and physical health through wellness-building activities such as writing and meditating during walks along the water, collecting journals, and playing tennis. LaToya's current dedication is also providing the blueprint for a publishing company, additional books, and a non-profit organization for youth that will incorporate the arts as a tool in effectively processing pain while broadening exposure to methods that will develop a healthy mindset. LaToya will also offer the opportunity to gravitate to a higher level of thinking through her speaking engagements, customized retreats, and holistic wellness communities.

LaToya believes that life is a beautiful journey. We are constantly growing and striving to get better; I encourage you to engage with LaToya in whatever way works best for you!

Here is how you can read LaToya's literary contributions, learn more about her upcoming events, and grab the opportunity to partner with her!

Follow LaToya On Social Media:

Facebook: Author LaToya Nicole

Instagram: @solocoaching

Visit her website at: www.latoyanicoleinc.com

To connect with her privately, please email: latoyanicole@solocoaching.net

Thank You

I pray that something resonated with you, sparking deeper study and the desire to heal deeply.

Please show your support by:

- Leaving a review on Amazon
- Sharing the book with a friend
- Sharing the text on your social media platforms

I am here for those whose pain silenced them. May every reader find their voice, tell your story, and restore your soul.

-LaToya Nicole

Made in the USA
Columbia, SC
23 December 2022

74897220R00046